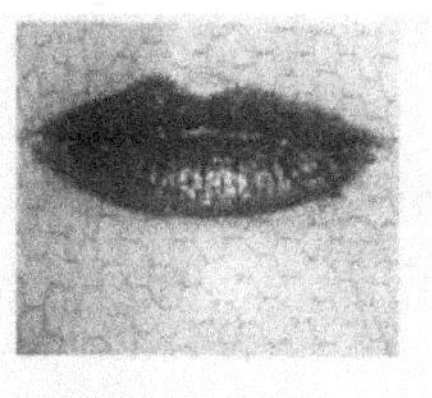

TO

KISS

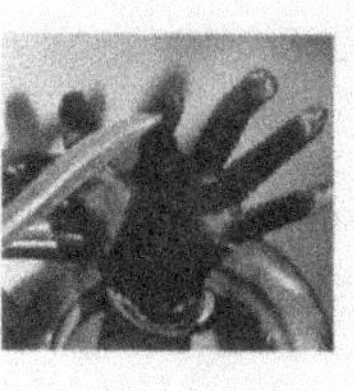
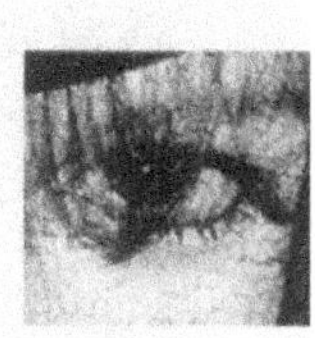

THE

BLOOD

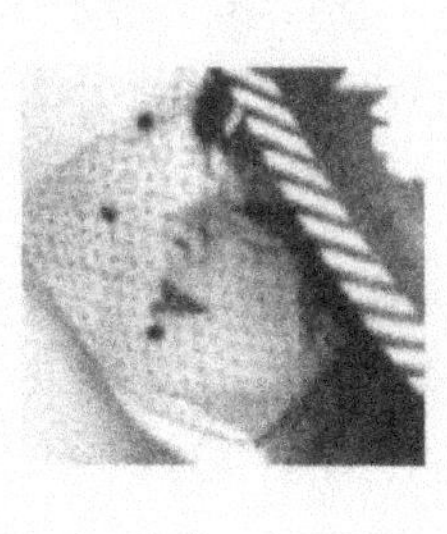

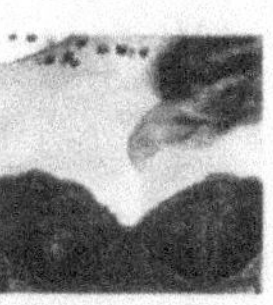

OFF

OUR

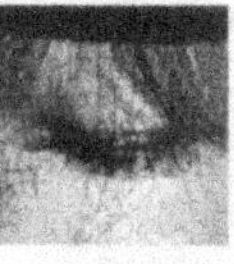

HANDS

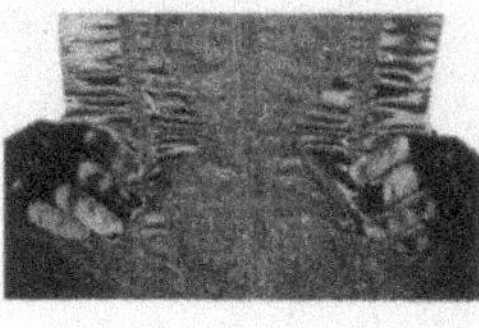

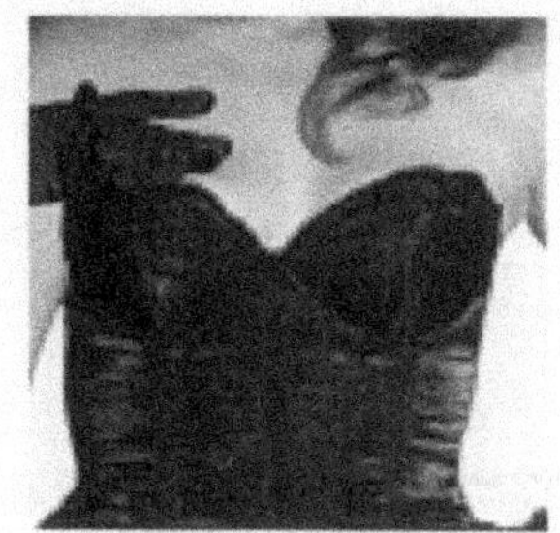
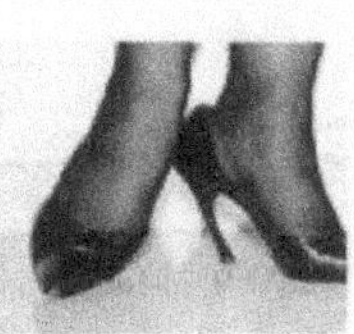

Acknowledging the following literary publications spoken word solo recording projects and compact disk compilations which were hospitable to most of what is collected here:

Angry Candy ▪ *Bachy* ▪ *Barney* ▪ *California Quarterly*
English as a Second Language ▪ *Fire Escapes*
Holy Doors ▪ *Italia /America* ▪ *Latino Stuff Revue*
Liquid Ohio ▪ *Motel Café* ▪ *Pearl* ▪ *Red Dance Floor*
Rio Grande Review ▪ *The Moment* ▪ *Sex in Public*
Sunset Palms Hotel ▪ *Wooden Head Review*
The Wormwood Review

Front cover, author photo & splash page graphics
Cynthia A. Duvall
Auteur wardrobe co-ordination
Tillie Aguilera
Cosmetic consultant, internal design & layout
Judith Orr

THE WOMAN:
Chase Masterson

Ion Drive Publishing
ISBN: 978-1-5168959-4-6

Dedication:

LAWRENCE WELSH
&
SCOTT DAVISON

WORD SURGEONS WHO HAVE
TRANSPLANTED THE MYTHIC
HEART OF TEXAS

Photo by Jimmy Santiago-Baca

L-R Scott Davison, Larry Welsh, Chris Gibson (Dallas, TX)

BLOOD SAMPLES

*It is the function of art to renew our perceptions,
because what we are familiar with we mostly
cease to see.*
— Anais Nin

*I am for an art that is brushed on a woman's mouth,
fixed to her thighs or slipped on her feet.*

— Claes Oldenburg

*My aim is to amuse, bewilder, annoy or to, simply,
inspire reflection.*
— Man Ray

TO KISS THE BLOOD OFF OUR HANDS

*If a painter needs a brush and a poet needs
a pen, then a film maker needs an army.*
— Orson Welles

The majority of police detection
Depends normally upon two
Ramifications: one of physical
Evidence and two: trace evidence

It's characterized by the blood trail
In 1940's psycho crime dramas referred
To (in German expressionist cinema
Tradition of despair desperation and
Brutality) as *Film Noir*

These elements of the art form impacted
Most of the mid-20th Century, plus us,
Along a long and winding path to the
Crimson boxoffice magnet of revival
House entertainment reflecting, even,
The more recalcitrant used women of
Urban cinema darkness

Coleen Gray, simply by her surname,
Becomes metaphoric in the shades
Of *gray* psychological gun-play ecstatic
Magic

Or we wait in the reeling dark battered
And wounded by the real world warfare
Outside

We have, all this time, been waiting for
Valli, Marie Windsor, Marsha Hunt,
Margaret Lindsay, Lizabeth Scott,
Myna Dell, Ella Raines, Paula Raymond,
Peggy Castle, Claire Trevor, Cleo Moore,
Beverly Michaels

The more dim their images are, now,
The more clear their curious poses in
Front of some recognizable cityscape
Backdrop

These are our dark places, where we
Moviegoers were allowed to enter, and
In our imaginations we were
Battle-scarred and bleeding,
Always waiting,
Waiting,
Waiting
For each one of these
Rare and barely remembered
Beauties to kiss the blood off our hands

SOMETIMES WE PROVIDE FOR OURSELVES OUR OWN HORROR

-- after Veda Ann Borg, her movies

The rain goes gray, as only it can
in a black and white fright flick. The
old broke bridge collapsed: just like
Carole Lombard's bed in the ironically
titled *Nothing Sacred.* The eerie screech

of *B.F. Goodrich:* a 4-door sedan is
racked-up on a mud flat; and 3 absent-minded
scientists, along with one sleek, hi-fashioned,
spun-gold-haired, hitch-hiker female tourist,
together stand, now, in the murky storm: all

the while brilliant lightning cracks the night
revealing this gloomy stone castle with
plenty of guest rooms. Vampires who
complain about working for scale kiss into
the necks of Harry Cohn's contract players.

Yet, nobody remembers you, Veda, except
maybe scabs like us waiting for non-union
labor and a pickup truck ride rattling off to a
day gig; those who stand in their own storms,
everyday, in *Blood City,* CA.

MEXICAN SPITFIRE

Dezilde que adolesco, peño, y muero
— **San Juan de la Cruz**
I got this piece of porcelain from Errol Flynn's bathtub
— **Harry E. Northup**

You think of Lupe Velez in the same light as
Estelita inside her skimpy Mexican tango drag,
But think a lot about her when the lights go
Off, too: extinguished like lit cigarettes which,
One time, threatened her veiled and fiery mouth
With death: in a way similar to that old drunk
Swashbuckler's bride Lili Damita, as she was
Rigged inside the same luminous international
Trappings.

Behind chic veil her porcelain face, like a single
Fragment from an actor's bathtub, reminds you
Of terrible histories clogging the brain drain.

It's tough to imagine her playing bits: **Mexican
Spitfire** you'd heard she referred to herself, once.
You forget why: but could she have been likened
To a variety of tiny Latino dragons? Maybe!

You can't help thinking about her when, all of a
Sudden, somebody reminds you that taking a dope
Kit to Mexico would be the same as bringing a bag
Of coffee beans to Brazil! Your immediate
Impression is that it's a place where she'd be alive,
At least, and wide awake.

FILM HEAD

after Robert Altman

Self-conscious merging traffic
through a *Movieola's* dissonant
sprocket-feed envisions a few
missing martyrs in a drug war
in Juarez. The border town is

trucker groan: cars and kidnapped
girls obscured by freeway rain.
Private imaginations are where grief
visits. And the sound is amazing in
the way the water dance an eaves

spout makes as it mixes with Annie Ross
singing **Farmer's Market** really becomes
its own damp counterpoint. So we listen
to the sprockets as poverty nibbles in our
pockets. All the while all these radiated

angels *madonna* the hair of whores,
and, as we *matador* strange bulls, they
congregate inside our skulls with a cast
of thousands. Whatever will be perceived
is a nihilist dissent in metaphoric dissolve

without mercy. It would seem as it is now
under queasy moonlight: a veiled attempt
to drown us ugly ducklings in the drear
blasphemous lake of very rich and utterly
whistling swans.

PICO BOULEVARD ILLUMINATION

we watch the middleclass suffer and die
in the **PEP BOYS** parking lot it's like

this guy says: *beautiful dog! beautiful
girl! what's its name? what's yr name?*

*what kind of a dog is it? is it a fun dog?
are you a fun girl?* finally the girl says:

*wait here a few moments. I'll get a leash
and a collar that will fit you perfectly!*

HAVING BRUNCH WITH LYDIA LUNCH

All the bowls have been broken like the
Hearts of teenage boys
In the cabs of Chevy pickups
Where the girls turn into toys

We're hungry over here at last
She hands us her napkin
Our recent demolition's past
Our souls all soaked in sin

All the waitresses were hooked
On a junkie guitar player
Out of the music store we walked
Now music doesn't have a prayer

Before we had a chance to be
Acquainted with this café
She wanted to slug the *maitre'd*
An undercover poet for the CIA

Que pasa woman we just don't see
Come on around to please explain
Why all this modern history
Is just so much ptomaine

Cookin' on the back burner we can use
A recipe of information you can't refuse
The 3 Stooges were proto-punk
Spike Jones was a new wave prophet

AN UNCONSCIOUS CRITIC LOOKS AT JAMES DOUGLAS MORRISON'S UCLA SCHOOL OF CINEMA ARTS DESIGN FILM

simple mortification of our senses: Cinco de
Maya; JDM takes Talia C. Dennis J. and me
into secret midnight screening: 16mm rolling
bathtub omens: strip poker not a joker in the
deck: film editing bungalow: ceiling zero
our scene is panacea
like a purge inside: popping lightbulbs
with a broom handle only a preview
of coming attractions: hot-shoe SS goosestep
below slow grind girl crossing her smoky
borders: tug of nylon war on a television
ballroom floor
high-heeled peepshow peek-a-boo pinup
girl dance: freedom dance: a tribal stomp
cut to women's gymnasium rooftop
speed camera action in the form of
Rilke's book: our hero is a page turner
look at his balancing act: shock value
transformation into schlock value
30 years down the road
movie-maker quit your trip
mid voyage your boat is over-ended
too stoned to see the sea
the sailor hiccupping home to
big screen ocean riptide
drowning in *Cinemathéque* Sangria

*Jim Morrison, as I remember him being a
Florida dude wearing flood pants, running
celluloid through an old style Movieola {no
computerized digital conveniences then} in
one of those film editing cabins no longer
extant on the UCLA campus. If Morrison
had not succumbed to pop-music's anesthetics,
he might have turned out to be every bit the
lyric film-maker his heroes Godard, Bunuel,
Fritz Lang and Carl Theodore Dreyer had been.
What follows amounts to a few desert images
from my journal composed when Jim took some
troops to Tucson, at the end of the Sixties, to shoot
exterior footage on his hitch-hiker movie HWY.*

HIGHWAY RETROSPECT

The Lizard King comes into these
abstract insect island trenches, in
order to advance new armies bivouacked

with hand-held camera ammunition. His
partners are a street singer and a hired
gun. Deals of death about the sands of a

desert, as it becomes painted by a bloody
afternoon radiator amplified by seven leading
ladies with blood-red hair. And you wonder if

those critics with cunning cinema incorporations
will want to pretend their own hands around the
throats of seven strangled girls.

FOLLOWING MY FAVORITE FEMALE TEACHER'S WOUNDED FALL THIS DREAM BLEEDS FOR HER

Brilliant orange sundress: lacey white piping,
like the type this actress wore in ***Johnny Eager:***
Lana Turner with narrow stream of black
fishnet fascinator swept up in sweep of her

platinum hair. But this woman turns on
flashlights in her eyes, lets me see how lovely
my room really is: she looks at glossy photos
on my chamber walls: they inspire her to turn

the pages of her mental diary, as she explains
degrees of random violence on Quiet Street. She's
disabled by staggered speech, though recollecting
a scene of senseless confrontations in backyards

overgrown with escaped killers: good reason for
all manner of barricades being erected just below
a foothill barrage of phlox blossoms bordering the
boulevard between Virgin Avenue and intrusion

of the *Global Village Miniature Golf Course.*
She described watching saw'd-off shotgun arrivals
which were rather useless defense (she'd contended)
against everything most of the residents didn't have

any clear intention of preserving, anyhow. Soon,
it was only lame lumber supporting whatever
still surrounded the corner ceiling molding in
most houses. There were *homey* chimneys sending

soot and ashes up into the stupid sky. So, while
all this was going on, under stricken circumstances
probably for fade-in, fade-out reasons, one
bright orange sign with white trim is hanging

off a black bent nail on a post formerly used for
tetherball tournaments. Why are there still so many
thinking the criminal justice system is corrupt, the
judges are crazy and that juries are out to lunch?

Outside of This Could Be My Shining Hour, *the duet lyrics between Joan Leslie & Freddy Astaire are practically non-existent in the silver screen vehicle* The Sky's The Limit. *There is an almost anti-musical aspect to this film which includes an uncommon presentation w/uniquely dynamic staging around an Astaire solo song & dance debut of the Harold Arlen, Johnny Mercer evergreen:* Make It One For My Baby And One More For The Road.

HER MOVIE SHOES

Copper penny over the vamp. It will give
good and mortal fortunes to us, under the
limits of the sky. Holding hands with the
dancer she loses the urgent photographs.
Then, there's the army thing she never
pictured him doing; or being absent without
leave. Or never saw him exert the destruction
of a cocktail lounge at 2:45 in the morning.
Romantic air-raid strikes, when movies can
camouflage widows waiting out a war, while

wholesale murder sanctioned by the military
booms a fractured economy. *Why are we
always out-numbered,* asked the girl. *Just to
keep things even, I guess,* said the dancer.
There will be some who'll make the same
mistake: thinking this is just another toke
off an old wartime cigarette. The girl doesn't
even smoke. She's walking across the green
insensitive shrapnel of luck and money. The
dancer: he stands ubiquitous guard.

THE INDISCRETION OF
AN AMERICAN WIFE
– after Jennifer Jones

A neo-Neapolitan night girl gone slightly mad.

Another dysfunctional husband in the garbage can.

As she would cater parties pursuing adultery's
                                        clandestine vows,
He wants her bones to be the place where raving
                                        pitbulls browse.

ACTRESS IN THE EVERGLADES

Once, there was this childhood loss
of identity: projection light warmer
than a summer night in Davenport,

Iowa. After dark, her steamy mouth
melts in Cinemascope and the actor
who's taking my place is making it

impossible, because I'd wanted my
puerile fingers, just like flattened
popcorn boxes, to slice a ripping

cleavage on the screen. I pretended
I was the protagonist who makes out
with her to the max, in spite of those

imposing oppositions of Seminole
warriors and a warty slave trader with
a dialect like an inebriated Victor

Borge. I imagined her mahogany hair
uncoiling down a turnpike spine towards
the crotch of South Carolina. Now 38 years

later, during a commercially hacked-up
television re-run, all my earlier ecstasy's
being reduced, as if she'd just turned into

a melancholy housewife at Jenny Craig.
My imagination, in the middle of the night,
is as hot as the hull of a nuclear submarine.

And I leave the room
dripping, just like....
just like a Florida swamp.

Ingrid Bergman/s daughter
is studying lingerie fashion
design in Paris. Her college
thesis will survey the history
of underwear.
                    Life Magazine (1972)

A QUATRAIN FOR ISABELLA

You wanted to study her underwear
Because she studied it in school
And she'd whip you with something sheer
Because **blue velvet** would be too cruel

SHE WILL DRESS UP TO ROAM THE NIGHT
after Gina Gershon

You're one of the *girl in peril* images wandering
out of a transformed Jim Thompson potboiler
novel and your stilted ankles in stacked heels are
the necessary spike: a vindictive liquor in an,

otherwise, harmless libation. Your twin brother
puts a kiss into the arch of your nylon foot, as if
to memorize the map of sex indexed by your
memorial toes. He hears verbal jazz roll off your

hot *4th of July* tongue, which wants to probe this
metaphysical blackmailer's hunger for a chick
who wears a cop shield attached to her custard-
colored lingerie. Sheryl Lee knows this world

and that the fireworks will come later. It's as
though she were aflame in France: a romantic
dessert flambé in French lace, whose highlights
are full of the usual paranoid delusion. We watch

corset suspenders and tiny silver clips collect her
classic double borders: she cannot compete tonight
with you: a fiery rose lit-up like a candle in your
hair and ashes of violent small town burnt-out love.

CLEO MOORE'S LAST INTERVIEW

*with perception beyond those
of the more commonly known
1950's blonde B-movie ladies,
she is here presumed to speak*

Hollywood's lovely dark & deep, but I
have promises to break. Hugo Haas was here,
but I had miles to go, before assassination
squads, who won't give me the chance to
become the Lieutenant-Governor of Louisiana,
pull the final pistol & drop me in my soundstage

snowy tracks. Hugo listens to the storm, as it
gossips in gutters, where I'd been blonde bait
seamy black & white: all the way from Lake
Arrowhead to the Palos Verdes Peninsula. The
cool platinum & sentimental snow, once shroud
for my shoulders thins to rain & falls upon the

graves of my enemies. Hugo listens to the storm
& disappears behind hills of manufactured fog. I
guess I wouldn't worry so much about the graves
of my enemies, if I just didn't have to think about
the graves for all my friends..... & me.

PINKY'S BLUES

It happened to be a film with
racial tensions. Jeanne Crain's

eyelids close: her eyelashes
like screen-doors softly slamming

shut. As complaints of summer
nights against a 1948 noisy

blackness of white pride flickers
on the screen, you can see that

behind her eyes are these intrepid
boats that top the lakes *ofeys* sail

on at resort retreats: torpid shells
which bargain with these lacustrine

underworlds: and lifting magical
nets to catch, even, the invisible

catfish spaces around here, to
snatch at her face, now, beginning

to resemble some stereotypical
panache. Could it be that, like a

delusional crustacean, she scuttles
inside all of us, perhaps, identifies

with what appears to hang-on
baring similar escape claws? And

how, at this very moment, when
soundtrack music swells beneath

disturbed Caucasian waters with
runaway girl tenacity, does she

trap the trip?

A RONDO FOR LUDMILLA TCHERINA

1

Tell the people of Teruel to SHUTUP! The
silhouette of a gallows in the farm yard: we
see you go around several rural circles. We

are witnesses to the weed ritual. In the balcony
with us the slow ballet of dope smoke coils like
hazy ghost dancers in your pirouette of cinematic

exchange. We are underneath the place where
you wear another hat: POT! But it's always the
romantic scheme you devise giving us our

contact high. The fumes that take us up are
illegal. Rituals of the movie screen allow us
to get lost.

2

Our identities are like Indians in a renegade
ghost dance. We want to pirate you on half-dark
islands of treasured obscure actress burial. Surely

we exchanged our fantasies just like joints of
marijuana: imagining ourselves in some dream
in one of the half-dark comers of a long-forgotten

schoolyard: next to the best blonde speller in the
7th grade. All the while, vicariously, we want to
topple you over just like Attila the Hun.

3

Look at you spinning & reeling all rowdy across
the floor of a Russian cabaret & in this balcony
where they allow smoking ghosts we watch the

people of Teruel & there's this girl: blond braids
in the background who really looks like she knows
how to spell the word *pirouette*

HOT TEXAS MINUTE
another one for Merlin

only this time, Ricky,
you really got it right

this time it's El Paso: there's
an ancient line of freight cars

tracked along a narrow
siding: numb & dumb

RIDE THE MAN DOWN

almost 4 years
before *Bwana Devil*
it was Barbara Britton

who almost married
a fencepost range of
bandit marauders that's

the view anyway
through splintered
gables by gunshot

ricochet ambush the foreman
fell off his horse in the rain
cows are already on the *Hatcher*

as abused ranches at Indian Springs
and if I were old enough I could see
myself putting up fences

around Barbara Britton oh I coulda
and I woulda but I tripped
over my tricycle in the driveway

and scraped my innocent knees

PRIVATE EYES FOR YOU

he felt the kitchen Friday night in
Larchmont like an intimate jazz club
smoke grass overcast mainline dreams
delirious talk she's a canary booked
by mistake cannot cut the tunes of a
schizoid trio shooting candy in the can
between sets

he's crazy for this chick like a Pacific
Northwest farm kid feeding 4-H pets
in Snohomish

but she's hung on the song
she can't even sing

and he doesn't want to cause any trouble
so he's Bogie   he's Juli Garfield   he's
Charles McGraw   he's Cagney   Eddie G
Sterling Hayden   Dana Andrews   Alan Ladd
down to the last bullet of disillusion   down
to his last *don't don't please don't*
don't let me die in this gutter {gasp}
his riddled body the lite White Plains rain

PRIVATE DETECTIVES SLEEP WITH THEIR CLOTHES ON

A private detective always sleeps with
his clothes on, always keeps his shoulder
holster in evidence. With eyes on gat,
his ears remember bullets dreaming out

loud in waterfront conspiracies or back-alley
betrayal. His piece is bitter cold, even when
it's working. His brunette secretary is cool,
pouring herself into skin-tone silk. She will

drench his *Saturday night special* in some
wet-proof gallery of romantically handicapped
clients. Then he says: "This caper's got more
curves than a bean ball chucked in by Ryne

Duren." His deductions
always come
at the
end.

ANOTHER LOST HIGHWAY
after David Lynch

border patrols push the heads of
day and night together: push through
clattering freezing breezes

across Low Line Canal: and the
ripping shadows of Nevada cars clamor
in filling stations as a slate-gray

sky cracks open and the yolk of morning
splatters its Easter lamination where
GREYHOUND buses look like old

scorched suicide notes in giant
motel room ashtrays: yet we now
know we have been called cultural

anarchists (without weapons
without purpose without destiny)
in our wicked return to neglected

intermountain regions of the Pacific
Northwest: and we realize although
we have been tuned-up like brand new

engines (and trust also our sense
of direction) to discover that not
enough people care we are coming

BIO-NOTE:

Michael C. Ford was born on the Illinois side of Lake Michigan. His debut LP vinyl which was a sequencing of air-checks from alternative radio appearances *(Language Commando)* earned a Grammy nomination in 1987. His volume of selected poems *(Emergency Exits)* was honored with a 1998 Pulitzer Prize nomination. His poem *Vietnam / Peace Casualties* was nominated for a 2006 Pushcart Prize. He's been invited to lecture at several universities, to be a frequent instructor for the Pen Center West *Pen in the Classroom* program and to recite at various venues: many times with musical accompaniment.

www.ingramcontent.com/pod-product-compliance
Lightning Source LLC
Chambersburg PA
CBHW061446050726
47593CB00004B/1493